A BOOK OF
ORCHIDS

BY
DR. CARL WITHNER
ILLUSTRATIONS BY JUAN LUIS G. VELA

A FRIEDMAN GROUP BOOK

Published by GALLERY BOOKS
An imprint of W.H. Smith Publishers, Inc.
112 Madison Avenue
New York, New York 10016

ISBN 0-8317-6660-3

A BOOK OF ORCHIDS
was prepared and produced by
Michael Friedman Publishing Group, Inc.
15 West 26th Street
New York, NY 10010

Typeset by B.P.E. Graphics, Inc.
Color separations by Hong Kong Scanner Craft Company Ltd.
Printed and bound in Hong Kong by Leefung-Asco Printers Ltd.

CONTENTS

INTRODUCTION

Orchids are among the most exciting plant families—to find in the wild, to grow, to study, to show or judge, or just to look at. Their colors, varieties, and forms never cease to amaze! There are more than 25,000 species and more than 75,000 cultivated hybrids. It takes a while to know them, but this little book may give an idea of their special appeal, from the classic *Laeliocattleya* corsage orchid to the exotic *Paphiopedilum*.

Orchids are highly evolved botanically and show their specializations in a variety of ways: some externally, in the ways the flowers are formed and adapted to specific insects for pollination; others internally, in terms of their biochemical processes. We shall explore some of these for your pleasure and information, and you can appreciate their exotic beauty at the same time.

Orchids are found throughout the world in all but the Arctic and Antarctic circles. The orchids native to the northern temperate zones are small terrestrial plants that often grow in bogs or sometimes in woodland habitats. In the tropics, however, most orchids are epiphytes, that is, they grow perched upon the branches and trunks of trees, habitats that serve to raise them up off the forest floor and into the sunlight. They do not parasitize the trees, but only sit upon them with the other epiphytes: air plants, mosses, ferns, and a variety of other species. When transplanted to the greenhouse and conditions for cultivation, they must be grown in porous bark mixtures to duplicate their airy home perches.

Soil is much too compact for growing any but the orchids that originally came from it. Most ground-growing orchids transplant badly; therefore, they must be conserved in their natural locations. Most naturalists and collectors keep such locations secret, since many terrestrial orchid species are rare. Today the International Endangered Species Convention protects all orchids when it comes to trade, but little protects them from the deforestation processes that result from population pressures, particularly in the tropics.

Now, just what is an orchid? The botanical explanation is primarily concerned with the structure of the flowers. Regardless of their size or particular form, all orchids share certain components. The sepals are three outer parts that protect the bud. When open, they color-up like petals. Inside the sepals are the three petals. The lip, or labellum, is distinctly different from the other two petals. The lip is a result of the adaptation of the flower to a specific type of pollinator and is, in a sense, a "landing field" to accommodate the visitor. Finally, the stamens and carpels are fused together into a single structure called the column. The lip and column are so positioned that the pollinator, visiting the flower for the nectar, fragrant oils, or other food, contacts the pollen in the visit and carries it on to the next flower, thereby assuring cross-pollination.

Orchids have a unique vegetative form. Their stems, when swollen with storage tissue for water and food, are called pseudobulbs (not true bulbs). A spongy white layer over the roots, called the velamen, soaks up any water and nutrients available and passes them on to these storage areas.

The habitats of many orchids are surprising as well. They are able to live in their tree-top environments with occasional rain or just night dews to supply their liquid requirements. Some orchids, unbelievably, live on cacti in desert areas where there is no significant rainfall and only nightly condensation of moisture when the temperature drops.

The seeds of orchids are also unusual. They are tiny, almost dust-sized; there may be as many as 3 million in a single seed capsule, which can take several months to ripen. The orchid seed embryo is immature compared to more conventional seeds and has little stored food. In nature, the germinating orchid seed must set up housekeeping with a beneficial fungus, producing a delicate mycorrhizal association. The fungus supplies food for growth until the leaves develop and the plant becomes independent. In the laboratory, it is possible to duplicate the fungal effects with sugars, minerals, and even vitamins and hormones. Thousands of seedlings may thus be grown artifically, in comparison to the few that survive and grow in nature. There is no longer a dependence upon the critical mycorrhizal stage, and after their first one or two years in the cultures they are large enough to be ready for potting out and growing on to flowering. These steps, which can't be rushed, help explain the time, expense, and care required in raising orchids in cultivation. The process from seed to flower may require anywhere from three to seven or ten years.

Orchid cultivation began in the Orient, and Confucius (551–479 B.C.) was among the first orchid fanciers. His phrase, the "king of the fragrant plants," epitomizes the qualities considered desirable in orchids today—graceful leaves, perfumed smell, a certain elegance of habit. Confucius was referring to Chinese *Cymbidiums,* which are still favorites in the Orient.

The Greeks collected wild orchids for their medicinal properties according to what became the Doctrine of Signatures, the belief that plants showed by their structures how they could be used to treat various diseases. The Mediterranean terrestrial orchids had underground tubers in pairs, so they were presumed to be good for sexual difficulties. In fact, the word "orchid" comes from the Greek *orchis,* meaning testis. In his pharmacopoeia, the famous and influential physician Dioscorides told how the tubers could be used to beget either male or female children, or if used unwisely, to "stirreth up the lust." One can only imagine how many hundreds of orchids were destroyed over the centuries by followers of Dioscorides' advice. Medieval herbalists were still repeating Dioscorides' recipes in their "herbals," which were illustrated treatises on plants. The herbalists attempted to describe and illustrate all known plants, including orchids, but the Greeks' superstitions still prevailed.

The next significant developments in orchid history occurred in 1768, when botanists at Kew Gardens began cultivating orchids. Meanwhile, Europeans traveling abroad brought back odd orchid plants from Asia to grow in their overheated greenhouses called "stoves." The tough pseudobulbous plants were able to survive those voyages, which took two or three months or more. The actual "first" was likely a plant of the genus *Bletia,* which was sent from the Bahamas to the famous horticulturist Peter Collinson in 1731. Starting out in the form of a dried herbarium specimen, it proceeded to grow and flower the following year.

Since that time, orchids have continued to grow in numbers, popularity, and worldwide availability. In these pages, many genera of the Orchidaceae are presented. A variety of beautiful species within these genera are described, and a number of hybrids appear as well. They are presented alphabetically according to common name. Hybrid names serve as common names, followed by the genus and a selection name, which indicates parentage. The date of hybridization is also included, when known. Ordinarily, the genus name would precede the hybrid common name (e.g. *Phalaenopsis* Alfonso Ibarra), but the hybrids names have been shortened here for clarity. Only a few species of orchids have informal common names, and these vary both regionally and internationally. For those species orchids in this book that do not have common names, we've taken the liberty of either translating their Greek- or Latin-based names, or assigning a name based on the flower's history. Their scientific names follow. If you wish to obtain species plants, rely on their scientific names and you'll be speaking the universal botanical language.

Growing orchids is no longer a rich person's hobby. You don't need greenhouses to grow these stunning flowers. There are many that grow well on windowsills or under lights, and the plants are easily available for reasonable sums. Although some selected orchids may be very expensive, the newer techniques of cloning, plus the more usual production of orchids from seeds, help keep costs down.

If you've not grown orchids before, this little book may encourage you to join the thousands who already enjoy their fascinating beauty. But there's a real caveat here—if you have one orchid plant, you will want more! This volume shows you why.

Beautiful Oncidium

Oncidium
O. pulchellum

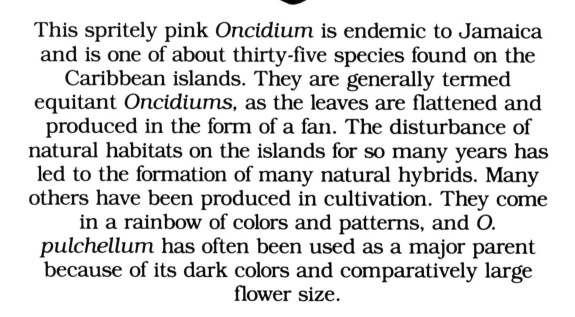

This spritely pink *Oncidium* is endemic to Jamaica and is one of about thirty-five species found on the Caribbean islands. They are generally termed equitant *Oncidiums*, as the leaves are flattened and produced in the form of a fan. The disturbance of natural habitats on the islands for so many years has led to the formation of many natural hybrids. Many others have been produced in cultivation. They come in a rainbow of colors and patterns, and *O. pulchellum* has often been used as a major parent because of its dark colors and comparatively large flower size.

BOCA DEL DRAGON

Encyclia

E. cordigera var. *alba*

~

This orchid was known for many years as the species *atropurpurea*, meaning a dark purple color, and then an older valid name was discovered referring to the heart-shaped lip. By now most people have changed the labels on their plants, but the other name is still used by some. It is a popular species and is found from Venezuela northward into Guatemala and Mexico. In Guatemala it is called *Boca del Dragon*. The sepals typically curl forward at their tips, a quality passed on to hybrids, and the color can vary from greenish with a maroon wash to dark rosy purple. The typical form has a white lip with a few purple lines at the base, but the lip on the variety *roseum* is purple overall. It has been cultivated in England since 1836, introduced by a Mr. Horsfall of Liverpool, an early orchid fancier.

BOSCHII

VANDA

V. luzonica x *V. tricolor*, 1928

This striking hybrid *Vanda* is a primary cross between two species, one from the Philippines, *V. luzonica*, and the other from Java, *V. tricolor*. It was registered as Boschii by the Munich Botanical Garden in 1928, when Latinized flower names were still popular. This is no longer possible by our present international rules for naming new hybrids, a procedure established to avoid confusion with botanical scientific names for plants. Both parents are reflected in the white flowers with magenta purple spottings, and they are extremely fragrant. The fully grown plant may have several stems, each of which can grow to about 3 or 4 feet, producing the many-flowered sprays. The plants have heavy, long roots that would attach them to trees if they were growing in nature. In cultivation they just hang in the air around the base of the plant.

Bouton d'or

BRASSOLAELIOCATTLEYA

Cattleya Wolteriana x *Blc.* Buttercup, 1968

These beautiful golden flowers result from several generations of breeding, and the cross has won many awards. It is noted for its good shape, long-lasting quality, and uniform color. The full wide lip comes from the *Brassavola* parentage, the shape and color from its *Cattleya* background, and its vigor from the *Laelia*. It is thus a multigenerational trigeneric hybrid and one of the best concolor yellow hybrids grown today.

BUTTERFLY ONCIDIUM

ONCIDIUM

O. papilio

~

Oncidium is a genus with a great variety of more than three hundred species in the New World. None is so unique or easily recognized as the group that includes the three Butterfly Orchids. The lateral petals and dorsal sepal look like the giant antennae of an exotic creature as the flower nods from its perch on the end of a long, curving stalk. The lateral sepals are colored like the lip. Although only a single flower blooms at a time, the stalk can continue producing flowers steadily for two or three years. The leaves are also attractive, being olive green strongly mottled in red. This species is found in Venezuela and Trinidad and has also been raised from seed in cultivation. It has been used as a parent in hybrids, but most prefer it just as a species. *Papilio* is the genus of the swallowtail butterfly, after which the orchid was apparently named when it was introduced in England in 1824.

CANTATA

CYMBIDIUM
Early Bird x Sicily, 1966

~

This *Cymbidium* is one of the hybridizers' attempts to produce a plant that will flower in the fall instead of the winter, when most *Cymbidiums* are in bloom. *Cymbidiums* come in a variety of colors, mostly pastel pinks, creams, greens, and whites, but breeders are trying to produce reds and other more vibrant tones as well. Since there is a whole range of miniature *Cymbidium* species available, the new hybrids, such as this one, are also smaller in size. As a result, four to six plants can be grown in the same space as one large, standard type. The Chinese and Japanese have grown the miniature types for hundreds of years.

CULMINANT

'LA TUILERIE'

LAELIOCATTLEYA

Ile de France x Gaillard, 1957

Modern hybrids of *Laeliocattleya* have more intense color as a result of breeding and selection, and more vigor and floriferousness than the parental species could show. This hybrid represents seven generations of hybridizing, approximately fifty years, to get its dark color, full shape, and fine lip, and it has won awards for its French originators, the company of Vacherot & Lecoufle. The flowers are sweetly fragrant on the plant, but as with other orchids they lose their perfume once cut, thus giving the impression that orchids lack fragrance. Many, if not most orchids do have it!

DIGBY'S
RHYNCHOLAELIA

RHYNCHOLAELIA

R. (Brassavola) digbyana

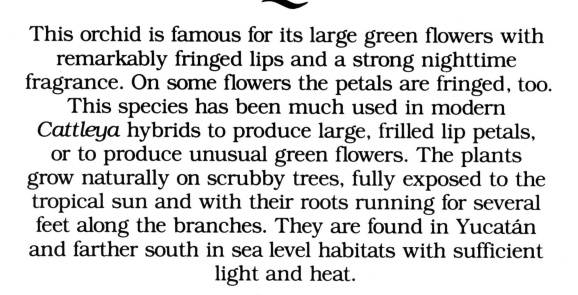

This orchid is famous for its large green flowers with remarkably fringed lips and a strong nighttime fragrance. On some flowers the petals are fringed, too. This species has been much used in modern *Cattleya* hybrids to produce large, frilled lip petals, or to produce unusual green flowers. The plants grow naturally on scrubby trees, fully exposed to the tropical sun and with their roots running for several feet along the branches. They are found in Yucatán and farther south in sea level habitats with sufficient light and heat.

DORIS HUNTER

PAPHIOPEDILUM

Doris Stanton x Mildred Hunter, 1949

Spotted green and brown lady's slippers are not liked
by all orchid growers, some of whom call them
"toads." Such epithets hardly reflect their strange
beauty. They are descended from several different
species of Indian lady's slippers, the most dominant
of which is *Paphiopedilum insigne,* which
contributes the spotted pattern to the hybrids. The
flowers often appear waxed or varnished, but the
high gloss is natural and enhances their beauty.
They come from cliffs and crevices in mountain
forest areas, so require cool conditions for cultivation.
They bloom from late fall into winter and have been
grown for years as ideal houseplants on a shady, cool
windowsill.

DWARF FIRE ORCHID

RENANTHERA

R. monachica

Renanthera is a tropical Asiatic genus with usually large and robust plants that may climb many feet into trees, reaching for the full tropical sun for flowering. But this species from Luzon in the Philippines is the baby of the genus, growing only 1 or 2 feet in height. That, naturally, makes it more popular than its 10-foot relatives for greenhouse culture. The Fire Orchids flower in a spray. The flowers are unusual in that the sepals are larger than the petals and the lip is the smallest part of all—just the reverse of the normal arrangement of an orchid flower. Also, the lateral sepals are nearly parallel. All the flowers of this group are bright red or orange with spottings of dark red, so they always make an intense color mark wherever they grow, usually the hot, humid areas near the Equator. These conditions are hard to provide in the greenhouse, so they are best cultivated outdoors.

Flower oF

San sebastiaN

Cattleya

C. skinneri var. *alba*

~

The national flower of Costa Rica, the Flower of San Sebastian is called *guaria morada* in Spanish and has appeared on stamps and money, as collectors well know. This is a rare white form of a usually purple species and has been found only a very few times in nature, three or four perhaps. Now, more are being produced in cultivation by self-pollinating the white flowers for seed. This species is often used for producing spring-flowering hybrids with clusters of flowers on multiple growths. A specimen plant after ten years may be a meter across with 35 to 40 flower heads and 300 to 400 blooms—a magnificent sight.

GENE PAGE FLEET

PAPHIOPEDILUM
Diversion x Walter Moore, 1970

~

This lady's slipper is a hybrid characterized by the cool-growing Indian species in its background. The dorsal sepal of the flower is particularly outstanding with its wide, flat shape and distinct veining. The division of color in the petals is typical, with the lower halves a paler color than the upper. The bosslike shield-shaped structure in the center is the modified third stamen of the flower, the other two remaining functional behind it. No one quite understands its function, but it must aid in attracting pollinator bees. In each species this stamenode has a distinctive shape, and the hybrid is intermediate between them. The pouchlike lip, or slipper, has in-turned upper margins to temporarily hold the bee and force it to brush against the pollen, which sticks to its back as it emerges, to be carried on to another flower.

GOLDEN GIFT

PHALAENOPSIS

Golden Buddha x Deventeriana, 1982

Hybridizers have been trying to produce a yellow *Phalaenopsis,* especially one without spots, for a long time; but since the two characteristics are seemingly inherited together, crosses like this one are the usual result. They are attractive in their own right, but there are never more than two or three flowers in bloom at the same time, and they are usually smaller in size than those of the parent plants. If these flowers are pollinated to make seed, the petals turn green, become more fleshy, and remain on the fruit, helping to produce food for the developing seed. So many crosses were being registered with the Royal Horticultural Society that they will accept no more names starting with "Golden." No one seems interested in emphasizing the spots!

Halawa beauty

Dendrobium
Calvin Morioka x Dora Zane, 1968

~

This hybrid was registered by Tanimoto from Hawaii in 1968. It is a so-called intersectional dendrobe hybrid that combines rather distantly related parents in a new combination. The long sprays are produced at the top of thick stems. These orchids generally like heat and humidity, so they do well under Hawaiian conditions out-of-doors as borders or in patio containers, where they can reach amazing size. The flowers last for several weeks, even when cut, and are readily sold by florists for bouquets and arrangements. The violet-purple color is a little unusual, as it is more ordinarily plain purple or green and brown in this category of orchids.

HARRY DUNN

SCHOMBOCATTLEYA

Cattleya Rowena Prowe x *Schomburgkia lueddemanniana*, 1955

Schomburgkia is a genus of large-growing plants with long wandlike stalks bearing terminal tufts of flowers. The blooms are usually crisped and floppy. These plants enjoy heat and sun, growing at sea level in Central America and northern South America, and are as tough as they come. By crossing with *Cattleya*, the plant size is brought down to a reasonable stature and the flowers are improved in color and shape. They still tolerate rough growing conditions, so make good candidates for outdoor culture in Florida and in tropical gardens.

HAYNALD'S PAPHIOPEDILUM

PAPHIOPEDILUM

P. haynaldianum

~

Haynald's "paph" belongs to a small group of lady's slippers that regularly produce two to six large spreading flowers on a long stalk, though they may not all be open together. This species was first discovered by Gustav Wallis in 1870 and was introduced by Veitch in England for cultivation in 1873. It came from San Isidro, near Manila, in the Philippines and is named after Cardinal Haynald, an archbishop of Hungary who also was a botanist. The plants can grow into fine specimens bearing numerous flowers on several stems, and they flower from January through March.

JEWEL BOX

SOPHROLAELIOCATTLEYA

Cattleya aurantiaca x *Slc.* Anzac, 1962

~

This is one of our most popular red hybrids today and has both orange and yellow flowers in its lineage. The red, however, comes from the miniature species of *Sophronitis coccinea* from Brazil, as does its smaller-than-usual plant size and its habit of producing multiple growths. Until recently, good red, full, flat flowers have been difficult to achieve, but Californian and Japanese orchid breeders have made the breakthroughs by using a red hybrid that was created in England in 1922, *Sophrolaeliocattleya* Anzac by name. Red hybrids have always been in great demand and have been expensive and hard to get, but now several new ones have been produced. Two especially fine forms of Jewel Box, 'Scheherazade' and 'Dark Waters,' have been propagated by cloning (meristemming) techniques, thus making the plants generally available at reasonable prices.

LADY OF THE NIGHT

BRASSAVOLA

B. nodosa

~

The Lady of the Night orchid is fragrant only after dark and can perfume a whole room. Pollinated by night-flying moths, this particular species is found in Central and South America. The fragrance disappears if the plant is exposed to light. A good species for beginners to grow, it is tolerant of light and heat and in nature may even be found growing near the sea on rocks that get salt spray. One never tires of its sturdy floriferous qualities, so it is found in nearly all collections today. It is much used as a parent to make colorful starry-flowered hybrids and is dominant as far as flower shape is concerned.

LAELIOCATTLEYA
CORSAGE ORCHID

LAELIOCATTLEYA

Laelia x *Cattleya*

~

Laeliocattleyas, crosses between *Laelia* and *Cattleya,* typify the quintessential orchid. This is the classic orchid for corsages, and is all too often worn upside down. As a result of breeding and selection, modern hybrids have more intense color, and more vigor and floriferousness than the parental species could show. This hybrid represents generations of hybridizing to get its unusual color, full shape, and fine lip.

LITTLE MISS MUFFET

CATTLEYA
C. guttata x Prospector, 1974

~

Pink is a difficult color to achieve in *Cattleya* orchids as it is usually tinged with lavender or purple. Surprisingly, this combination worked out well for the hybridizer in that the color is clear, and yet one of its parents is a green-bronze color with spottings of magenta. This hybrid has bifoliate *Cattleya* characteristics in the tall stems with double leaves, and a name to match the pert flowers. This type of *Cattleya* was once known as a "cocktail" orchid, because the medium-sized flowers were good for afternoon corsage wear, but, need I say, little heed is paid to such amenities any more.

MALONES

'FANTASY'

DENDROBIUM
Akatuki x Glorious Rainbow, 1973

～

This hybrid dendrobe is descended mainly from *Dendrobium nobile,* a popular orchid species from India that is used extensively for breeding because of its easy culture and floriferous habits. Various chromosome races of these plants have been found, and now the pentaploid hybrids, such as this one produced by the Yamamoto family, are being grown commercially in Japan and Hawaii for their large flowers which come in a kaleidoscope of colors. They are sold as elegant potted plants for midwinter holiday occasions. The flowers will last for six weeks, and a well-grown specimen may have forty to fifty blooms completely covering the stems from top to bottom—very showy indeed! These make good houseplants in cool, sunny windows and can go on from year to year, so enjoyment of their perfection is not limited to greenhouse growers. The 'Fantasy' clone of the hybrid was singled out for a special name because of its fine color and shape.

MAUDIAE

PAPHIOPEDILUM

P. callosum x *P. lawrenceanum*, 1900

From the mottled-leaved, warm-growing lady's slippers of Thailand and other parts of southern Asia, many hybrids have been produced in cultivation. Maudiae is the hybrid of two albino parents that lack the normal red and brown pigmentation that usually colors the flowers of the species. It was first registered with the Royal Horticultural Society in 1900. The green and white striping produces an intriguing color combination that makes it as popular today as when it was originated. It may be found in nearly all orchid collections. These *Paphiopedilums* are easy to grow into specimen plants, even on a windowsill or under lights, and a full pot may produce five or six flowers. As with other *Paphiopedilums*, the flowers may last for two months in perfect form. The plants require somewhat warmer growing conditions than the cool-growing Indian species with solid green leaves.

ORANGE CATTLEYA

CATTLEYA

C. aurantiaca

This is a tolerant species found in Mexico and Central America. It is relatively common and tolerates exposure to sun and heat, desirable characteristics it passes on to its many hybrids today. In addition, it is floriferous and contributes to the production of red, orange, and yellow flowers. It also hybridizes in nature with *Cattleya skinneri,* the national flower of Guatemala, to produce *C. guatemalensis,* which varies from red and orange to salmon and purple and even, rarely, to yellow and white. Certain Central American areas produce a type of self-pollinating flower that forms clusters of seedpods without even opening. Needless to say, these types are not as desirable horticulturally as the others. It is possible to grow fine specimen plants of *C. aurantiaca,* and a recent award-winner was about a meter across with hundreds of flowers in neat orange heads.

PALM-POLLY

POLYRADICION

P. lindenii

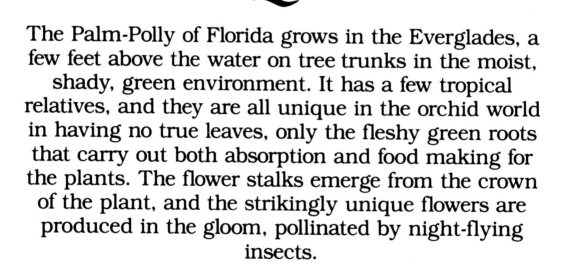

The Palm-Polly of Florida grows in the Everglades, a few feet above the water on tree trunks in the moist, shady, green environment. It has a few tropical relatives, and they are all unique in the orchid world in having no true leaves, only the fleshy green roots that carry out both absorption and food making for the plants. The flower stalks emerge from the crown of the plant, and the strikingly unique flowers are produced in the gloom, pollinated by night-flying insects.

PARISH'S VANDOPSIS

Vandopsis

V. parishii

Vandopsis is a genus from Burma and Thailand
with strange spotted flowers that are fleshy green
with a red lip. There also occurs a completely
maroon colored variety of the species with
rounder-shaped flowers, all of the spots coalescing so
that the darker color blocks out the green. Recently
these flowers have been used to hybridize with
Vandas and other Asian orchids to produce flowers
with new forms and colors, especially reddish tones.
The plants have very fleshy, hard, leathery leaves.
This species was discovered in Moulmein in 1862 by
the Reverend Parish and sent back to England for
cultivation.

PRIMROSE DENDROBIUM

DENDROBIUM

D. primulinum

~

Dendrobium is one of the largest genera throughout tropical Asia, Australia, and the South Pacific islands, particularly Papua New Guinea, with hundreds of species. Some of the showiest, with brightly colored hanging flowers, are from the hills of northern India. Some individual flowers of some species can last as long as six months (another orchid record!) and others may last only a few hours, less than a day. Many, like this species, are seasonal growers, growing in the wet, warmer time of year and losing their leaves completely to flower from the bare stems in the drier, cooler season. Altogether a remarkable group of species taking advantage of every ecological niche! The general appearance and fragrance of the flowers must have reminded the discoverer of primrose.

ROSY-COLUMNED
AERANGIS

AERANGIS

A. luteoalba var. *rhodosticta*

This orchid is tricky to grow, but the pretty white flowers with red columns make it an instant favorite. It comes from Kenya, Uganda, the Congo, and nearby areas, and grows on forest trees in warm, moist locations near rivers or waterfalls. A fine specimen can be grown, with multiple sprays, and the plants always do best when mounted on a branch or slab of cork so the roots can be exposed. *Aerangis* is an African-Malagasian genus with more than seventy species; almost all have white flowers with nectar spurs hanging from the lips. Most are pollinated by moths with long tongues that can reach the nectar.

SANGUINE BROUGHTONIA

BROUGHTONIA

B. sanguinea

～

A species endemic to Jamaica, this *Broughtonia* varies in color from a deep blood red (after which it is named) to lighter shades of rosy purple. More recently, all-yellow and all-white forms have been discovered, and they are very much in demand. The plants require much humidity and sun and are tough and leathery with long roots attached to the tree trunks or fence posts where they may grow in nature. The plants observe a definite winter dormancy when they should not be watered very much in cultivation. In summer, the flower stalk may rebranch, extending the blooming season to nearly a year. A fine specimen clump can produce several stalks and form a whole sunburst of bloom. The bright, rounded, flat flowers are popular in modern hybridizing with *Cattleyas,* which usually produce miniature red-flowering plants. They can be real spotlights of color and are always at a premium. The genus is named after Arthur Broughton, an English botanist, and was introduced at Kew in 1793.

SCARLET SOPHRONITIS

SOPHRONTIS

Sophronitis coccinea (grandiflora)

～

A native to the cloud-shrouded forests of coastal Brazil, this *Sophronitis* is used for breeding modern red hybrids of miniature plant size. In nature, these flowers shine like spotlights in the forests, and make equally showy specimens in the cool, moist greenhouse. Some Japanese orchid growers specialize in this species alone, and may have as many as 500 specimens, or more, in a small greenhouse.

SPARKES' CYMBIDIUM

CYMBIDIUM

C. canaliculatum var. *sparkesii*

~

Another inhabitant of warm, or even hot, areas, this orchid is found in northern Australia and down into inland regions of eastern Queensland to New South Wales. The plants grow on trees and have tough, leathery, upright leaves. The sprays of flowers hang down below the leaves. Flowers vary in color from clear green, the so-called *alba* variety, to spotted, to a solid, deep red-brown in variety *sparkesii*. In fact, from a distance, the flowers can appear black, but they are not. (Black flowers don't really exist, except in myth and the literary imagination, or the popular "Brenda Starr" comic strip. They are very dark purple or red, usually with a velvety surface that doesn't reflect light—thus causing the illusion.) The plants are not easy to grow in cultivation, but the display is well worth it when they do well.

WINGED ENCYCLIA

ENCYCLIA

E. alata

~

A typical pseudobulbous-stemmed *Epidendrum* type, this Winged *Encyclia* was found by G. Ure Skinner in 1837 in Honduras. Afterward it was found in Mexico and other Central American countries. The flowers are sweetly fragrant and vary in color from an olive green to nearly brown. The orangy yellow ruffle on the front edge of the lip and the clear yellow lateral lobes are its hallmarks. Hybridizers are gradually realizing that it makes a good parent with *Cattleyas* or *Laelias*, as the large flowers, ruffled lip, and the red veinings are all desirable qualities. In addition, it is easy to grow and flowers freely. In all ways, a good plant to have around!

ORCHID CULTIVATION

It has been said, "If you can grow ferns, begonias, or African violets, you can grow orchids." In many ways this is true. These plants all require, within narrow limits, specific light conditions and a relatively high humidity for successful culture. Two points often overlooked, though, are getting to know what kinds of orchids are available and choosing plants that will flourish under the conditions that *you* can provide.

You will want to talk with other orchid growers, perhaps join a local society to see their show-table, and, most important, read some of the great numbers of available books and magazines that highlight orchid cultivation. Many times at orchid shows or society meetings beginners' plants are available for sale at reasonable prices. It is good to start out with three or four mature plants of various kinds. Find out by trial and error which will flower best for you. Growing orchids requires patience and experience, but with a few plants you should have at least one that will always be "doing" something—new lead growths of shoots or roots, leaves developing, flower stalks arising, blooms opening. Some orchids have dormant periods when only the status quo is apparent and no new growth or development is occurring. When you've gained some experience with mature plants, you can begin to experiment with growing seedlings. You should expect that it will take from one to two years for new plants to adapt to their surroundings and really come along; this depends, of course, on how "green" your thumb may be.

Orchids have the same basic growth requirements as do all plants, but the appropriate combination of these factors is often more critical for orchid cultivation than for other plants. These factors include proper temperature, good light, adequate humidity, continued air circulation, suitable potting material, methodical watering, balanced fertilizing, and freedom from pests and diseases. The supply of good light and sufficient humidity are often the most critical elements in home orchid growing.

Three temperature categories for orchids are recognized: cool (50°–55°F.), intermediate (about 60°F.), and warm (65°–70°F.). This refers to nighttime temperatures. A 10 to 15 degree differential between night and day is a necessity for successful orchid culture. Intermediate orchids match our own living requirements well, though a cool windowsill or northern exposure can be used for the cool types. Try any of the following, as they are good beginners' plants that can grow and flower under either cool or intermediate conditions: *Brassavola nodosa, Cattleya aurantiaca, Epidendrum cochleatum, Dendrobium nobile, Paphiopedilum villosum, Oncidium sphacelatum* or *Oncidium maculatum.* Warm growers, such as *Phalaenopsis* species or hybrids, or the spotted-leaved lady slippers are especially good for culture under lights or in a warm, south-facing room. A large standard or a small miniature cymbidium will do well on a well-lighted, cool sunporch or bay window. Sometimes moving the plant from one window to another will make a difference until you discover the combination the plant likes best.

Light is sometimes more important than temperature, and light often controls the other variables that affect whether your plant flowers or not. Most orchids enjoy good light and prefer growing in a southern or eastern exposure, sometimes directly in the sun. Morning light is preferred over the hotter noon and afternoon beams that can dehydrate the plants. If the leaves turn yellow, the plants may be receiving too much light and their growth will be stunted. If the plant growths are soft and floppy, too dark a green, and without flowers, the orchid is probably not getting enough light. If each new growth is larger than the previous one, and, once mature in size, a number of flowers are produced, then you've given your orchid proper care.

Humidity, as distinct from watering, should fall between 50 percent and 60 percent—or even 70 percent—so misting the plants at midday or midafternoon is often desirable. Or, have them growing with other plants or with a humidifier. It will make the air more comfortable for you too, especially if you have hot-air heat. The results of sufficient humidity will provide well-expanded leaves and pseudobulbs, well-opened flowers, and aerial roots that continue their growth over the edge of the flowerpot.

You should take care when you water the plants, drenching the potting material once or twice a week; dormant orchids or those with tough pseudobulbous stems and leaves need watering less often than the others. Just be certain that the plants have dried off by evening when the temperature goes down—no liquid drops should remain on or at the leaf angles where a rot could begin. A little fertilizer added to the water, about one-quarter the amount specified, is desirable; you can increase the amount a little when very active growth occurs.

Plastic pots are used often today, but some growers still prefer to use clay pots, though the clay pots—especially if small—dry out more quickly. The clay containers are often placed on racks over pans of wet gravel to increase the humidity. Orchids need repotting every two or three years into new mix—whatever kind you may find available: coarse, peaty compost; mixtures of bark, coarse pumice granules, and charcoal; crushed lava rock; coarse fern roots of various sorts; or sometimes sphagnum moss—just no soil. The mixtures must be long-lasting, porous, and well-drained so the orchid roots with their velamen layers receive plenty of air. Remember you are, most of the time, trying to duplicate conditions on a tree trunk in the tropics.

Finally, don't be intimidated or afraid to experiment! Orchids grow slowly and they die slowly. If things don't seem right, change the conditions. All growers—even the experts—have killed a few plants in their time. When your first flowers come along, you'll be more than pleased! And then you'll want another plant—and another.

GLOSSARY

AERIAL ROOT
A root that hangs from the stem into the air unattached to a support. Common on many epiphytes and climbers in the tropics.

CALYX
A collective term for all the sepals of a flower.

CANE-TYPE
Having a coarse upright stem that is strong but still fleshy and looking like a short section of sugar cane or similar plant.

CARPEL
The female organ of a flower, a unit or section of the fruit or pod that bears seeds inside. There are three carpels in orchid fruits.

CLONING
Reproducing the same plant repeatedly by vegetative techniques with cuttings, budding, grafting, divisions, etc., or by microscopic tissue culturing or meristemming techniques in the laboratory.

COLUMN
The fused tissue combining both stamens and pistils, or their modifications, in the center of the flower.

COOL-GROWING
Requiring night temperatures around 50° to 55°F. and a moderate daytime environment.

CROSS
Mating two different parents to produce a new population.

CULTIVAR
A single plant selected from a species or hybrid population because of distinguishing quality of form or color; the same as the older term, *variety*, when used horticulturally.

EPIPHYTE
A plant that is growing upon another plant and that is physically supported by it but *not* parasitizing the host plant.

GENUS
A collection of closely related species in a given family of plants or animals.

INTERSECTIONAL
Hybrid made between species or hybrids representing two sometimes widely different species classified in different subgenera of a large genus.

LEAD
The new growth from the main dormant bud at the base of the preceding growth.

LIP (LABELLUM)
The special petal of the orchid flower that serves to help attract the pollinator. It is usually positioned and formed to be a "landing platform" and aid in the pollination process.

MERISTEMMING
A laboratory process employed to reproduce especially fine plants, usually genetically identical, by culturing the growing point (meristem) tissue from the stem tip of a given plant.

MULTIGENERIC
Referring to a hybrid plant with parents that are also hybrids, usually of different sorts, so that the offspring represent a combination of up to six genera in one.

MYCORRHIZA
The combination of a root and a beneficial soil fungus that grows on decaying organic matter, helping the root to absorb nutrients and providing certain organic compounds, especially sugars, vitamins, and amino acids produced by the fungal metabolism.

POLYPLOID
Having more than the usual two sets of chromosomes in the nucleus of each cell, usually three or four (triploid, tetraploid), but sometimes more.

PRIMARY CROSS
A hybrid produced by mating two different species (*see also* Multigeneric).

PSEUDOBULB
A usually spherical or pear-shaped, fleshy, hard stem of many orchids; a stem adapted for water storage.

REED-STEMMED
Having a tall, usually stiff and strong, stem that is only a few millimeters in diameter—as contrasted with cane-stemmed or pseudobulbous orchids.

SEPAL, DORSAL
Three sepals compose the calyx of a flower. This sepal is located opposite the lip petal and is usually the uppermost part of epiphytic orchid flowers.

SPUR
A nectar-containing tubelike extension from the base of the lip petal. It can be short and wide or long and narrow.

STAMEN
A male element that bears pollen grains in the flower.

TISSUE CULTURE
The growing of plant tissues in test tubes on a sterile nutrient medium and the propagation of new plants from such tissue.

VARIETY
An older horticultural designation for a plant distinguished in its population by fine color or form and usually given a name, in single quotation marks, for marking that distinction (*see also* Cultivar).

VELAMEN
A spongy multilayered epidermis on orchid roots that can temporarily absorb water or dissolved nutrients, passing them on into the root. The velamen can also attach the root to the tree or other substrate.